animal planet™

I Am Fungie the
DOLPHIN

Level 2

Written by Brenda Scott Royce

Silver Dolphin

PRE-LEVEL 1: ASPIRING READERS

 LEVEL 1: EARLY READERS

 LEVEL 2: DEVELOPING READERS

- Simple factual texts with mostly familiar themes and content
- Concepts in text are supported by images
- Includes glossary to reinforce reading comprehension
- Repetition of basic sentence structure with variation of placement of subjects, verbs, and adjectives
- Introduction to new phonic structures
- Integration of contractions, possessives, compound sentences, and some three-syllable words
- Mostly easy vocabulary familiar to kindergarteners and first-graders

 LEVEL 3: ENGAGED READERS

 LEVEL 4: FLUENT READERS

Silver Dolphin Books
An imprint of Printers Row Publishing Group
A division of Readerlink Distribution Services, LLC
9717 Pacific Heights Blvd, San Diego, CA 92121
www.silverdolphinbooks.com

ISBN: 978-1-64517-745-6
Manufactured, printed, and assembled in Rawang, Malaysia.
First printing, April 2021. THP/04/21
25 24 23 22 21 1 2 3 4 5

3

Dolphins live in oceans all over the world. We are excellent swimmers.

Some dolphins travel long distances, and go to different places.

Very few have a favorite spot like I do.

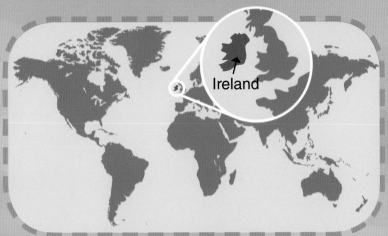

Ireland

This is Dingle. It's a village in southwest Ireland.

I spend a lot of time on my own in Dingle's **harbor**.

The tide brings lots of fish into the harbor. Fish are my favorite food.

Dolphins are very good at catching fish. We also eat squid, shrimp, crabs, and other small sea creatures.

Fishing boats come and go all day. Sometimes I chase them. It's fun to ride the waves.

Beyond the harbor is Dingle Bay. From there, it's a short swim to the Atlantic Ocean.

People come from around the world to see me. Some watch from the beach. Others cruise by on boats or rafts.

When I hear engines chugging and people calling, it's time to play!

Humans are such interesting creatures! I see their smiles when I swim past them. I hear their cheers when I flip and spin.

They squeal with delight when I splash them. It's a fun game!

Look at me!

With a powerful thrust of my **fluke**, I leap from the water. Up, up, up, fifteen feet or more.

When I can soar no higher,
I turn around and plunge
headfirst into the water.

People say I'm a bit of a show-off. It's true, sometimes I do like attention.

No one trained me to "perform," though. I'm wild and free! I do what comes naturally, and only when I feel like it.

In summer, a lot of people spend time in the water. They swim and take rides in canoes and kayaks. A lot of them come to say hello. If I'm in a playful mood, I'll join in the fun!

I may swim in circles or sneak up behind them. They don't hear me coming. Surprise!

In winter, the sea is cold. Fewer people come to visit.

My body has a layer of fat called **blubber** that keeps me warm.

Seals and seabirds also don't mind the cold. We play now and then.

Occasionally, an orca comes into Dingle Bay. Orcas can grow up to 30 feet long. That's more than twice as big as me!

Did you know that orcas are dolphins, too?

long-beaked common dolphin

hourglass dolphin

Atlantic spotted dolphin

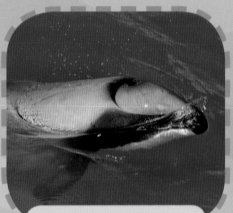

Hector's dolphin

There are more than 30 different **species** of dolphins. Here are just a few.

I am a bottlenose dolphin. We're known for our big brains and friendly smiles.

Our name comes from the shape of our **rostrum**. Can you guess what a rostrum is?

The Irrawaddy dolphin has a rounded head and a short rostrum.

The Amazon River dolphin's rostrum is long and slender.

Dolphins are **social** animals, and most travel in a group called a **pod**. Some pods have more than forty members.

As for me, I like the **solitary** life.

I always know when other dolphins are nearby. We "talk" to each other using clicks, whistles, squeaks, and squeals. We also **communicate** with body language and touch.

When I first came to Dingle, some people thought I was a shark. It's a common mistake.

SHARK
type of fish
can breathe underwater
breathes through gills
sharp teeth for cutting
teeth constantly replaced
tail moves side-to-side
excellent sense of smell

DOLPHIN

type of mammal

must surface to breathe

breathes through a blowhole

rounded teeth for grabbing

teeth are not replaced

tail moves up-and-down

no sense of smell

My **dorsal fin** helps me balance. It keeps me steady while I swim.

Scientists can tell dolphins apart just by our dorsal fins. They're unique, like human fingerprints.

Pollution is a growing problem for dolphins—especially plastic. Plastic takes hundreds of years to break down. Plastic waste clogs waterways and washes up on shore. Even here in Dingle.

To help dolphins and other **marine** creatures, you can try to use less plastic. Remember to recycle, too!

The people of Dingle look out for me.

One night, a ship crashed against the rocks. Oil leaked from the damaged boat, turning the water black. My human friends, worried the oil would make me sick, called to me, and I left the area and was safe.

I sometimes explore the waters beyond the harbor. But I always return.

There's no place I'd rather be.

I've loved my life in Dingle. I've made so many new friends and made so many people smile.

Take A Deep Dive with Dolphin Facts!

Dolphin teeth are designed for grabbing food, not cutting it. Dolphins swallow fish whole—and head first.

Dolphins sleep with one eye open. Half of the brain switches off while a dolphin dozes. The other half stays awake and aware.

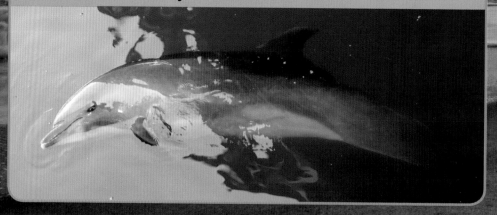

Bottlenose dolphins are speedy swimmers. They can reach speeds of up to 25 miles per hour.

Dolphins use **echolocation** to navigate and find food. They bounce sounds off fish and other objects in the water. The echoes tell dolphins the size and location of the objects.

Glossary

blubber: a layer of fat that marine animals use for warmth and energy

communicate: to share information, ideas, and feelings

dorsal fin: a fin on the back of a fish, shark, or whale

echolocation: using sound to "see" objects

fluke: a dolphin's tail fin

harbor: a protected body of water where ships and boats can dock

marine: living in the sea

pod: a group of dolphins, porpoises, or whales

rostrum: a dolphin's snout

social: prefers living in groups

solitary: prefers living alone

species: a group of living things different from all other groups